ALTERNATOR BOOKS™

DIGITAL SAFETY SMARTS

CHOOSING ONLINE SOURCES

Katie Clark

Lerner Publications ◆ Minneapolis

Dedicated to my loves, always.

Lerner Publications Company
An imprint of Lerner Publishing Group, Inc.
241 First Avenue North
Minneapolis, MN 55401 USA

For reading levels and more information, look up this title at www.lernerbooks.com.

Main body text set in Aptifer Sans LT Pro
Typeface provided by Linotype.

Library of Congress Cataloging-in-Publication Data

Names: Clark, Katie, 1983–author.
Title: Choosing online sources / Katie Clark.
Description: Minneapolis : Lerner Publications, 2025. | Series: Digital safety smarts (alternator books) | Includes bibliographical references and index. | Audience: Ages 8–12 | Audience: Grades 4–6 | Summary: "Fake news and biased sources abound in the digital world. Readers discover how to use critical thinking to sniff out unreliable sources, as well as tips for including balanced views in their research"—Provided by publisher.
Identifiers: LCCN 2024048611 (print) | LCCN 2024048612 (ebook) | ISBN 9798765668245 (library binding) | ISBN 9798765683835 (paperback) | ISBN 9798765676370 (epub)
Subjects: LCSH: Media literacy—Juvenile literature. | Internet literacy—Juvenile literature. | Fake news—Juvenile literature.
Classification: LCC P96.M4 C53 2025 (print) | LCC P96.M4 (ebook) | DDC 302.23/1—dc23/eng/20241209

LC record available at https://lccn.loc.gov/2024048611
LC ebook record available at https://lccn.loc.gov/2024048612

Manufactured in the United States of America
1-CG- 7/15/25

TABLE OF CONTENTS

INTRODUCTION

NOT A RELIABLE SOURCE

Kyle and Poppy settled onto the couch in the living room. They huddled close to the laptop because they had a science project coming up, and they were class partners.

"Do you think airplanes are a good topic?" Kyle asked.

"Of course!" Poppy said. "Airplanes are the best."

"You're just saying that because your mom is an aircraft mechanic."

Poppy smiled. "Maybe."

They fell into silence as they read about the way airplanes work. Kyle clicked on an interesting-looking link.

"Wow!" he said. "Did you know that airplanes experience turbulence because they're about to crash?"

When searching for online sources, make sure that they are reliable.

Poppy frowned. "I don't think that's true. My mom says that turbulence is pretty normal."

Kyle pointed to the screen. "It says it right here!"

Poppy checked out the online blog he had pulled up, and she shook her head. It just looked like some random person's opinion posted online. "That's not a very reliable source," she said.

"What's a reliable source?" Kyle asked.

"It's a source you can trust to provide correct, well-verified information," she explained. "It's proven to give you accurate information about a subject. Like my mom with airplanes."

"Oh," Kyle said. He clicked the X to close the page. "So I probably shouldn't keep reading information on that blog."

"No," Poppy agreed. "Probably not."

CHAPTER ONE

UNDERSTANDING RELIABLE SOURCES

Knowing how to find the information you need is an important life skill. Kyle and Poppy were looking for online sources for a school project, but people use research in many different ways.

What Makes a Source Reliable?

A source is anything that provides information. Two kinds of sources exist. One is a reliable source. This means the information comes from an expert's experience and opinions. Or it could be a source that has a good reputation for using correct facts.

The other kind is an unreliable source. This is a source that doesn't have any professional knowledge, education, or training in the area it's talking about. It might say information that is not accurate, or even make up false information.

The best kind of source to use is a reliable source. Official websites, medical journals, and educational databases are a few examples of reliable sources. You should avoid unreliable sources such as blogs, opinionated articles, or sources that only focus on one person's or group's point of view.

SEARCH ENGINES

Have you ever used a search engine? These handy online tools let you type in a subject and then they provide you with a lot of possible answers. Choose your search tools wisely!

Evaluating a Source

How can you check a source's credibility? One way is to figure out who created the information and why. This will help you decide if they are an expert in the field.

Imagine you're looking for the best beach for swimming. You do a web search and click on a blog that strongly recommends a beach a few miles away. You get there only to discover the beach is strewn with garbage!

When you look up the author who recommended this beach, you see that they own a resort further down on the beach that allows public use of its clean beach for a fee.

Using sources that are unreliable might mean that searching for a beach to visit takes you to a place like this.

The 5 W's of Evaluating Sources

Who wrote this?

What subject are they talking about?

When was this written?

Where was this written?

Why did the author write this?

He probably wrote the article in order to get more business. You quickly realize that if you had researched the author first you would have known this wasn't a very reliable source for good beaches. This is just one example of why finding a reliable source is an important skill.

Types of Sources

Lucky for us, we can find reliable sources in a lot of ways. When you're looking for information, check out websites, news outlets, magazines, and books. A library is a great resource for research! Librarians can even help you with online research.

When searching for reliable sources at the library, librarians are great people to ask for help.

Look for sources that specialize in their subject matter. Make sure any news outlets you read have a good reputation and are unbiased. This means they don't change or hide information to fit their own purposes or point of view. Books published by professionals are also a good resource. These are all primary sources.

Make sure you look for at least a couple of primary sources when you're looking for information. This means a source that has information from eyewitness accounts or experts on the subject. Secondary sources have information from second-hand accounts. These should be used only as support for information found from primary sources.

An interview with an eyewitness is a good primary source.

CHAPTER TWO

FACT-CHECKING AND SPOTTING FAKE NEWS

Unreliable sources come in many different forms. One of the most common is called fake news.

What is Fake News?

Fake news is tricky business. It is meant to mislead people into believing false claims. Fake news is mostly found online, but it can also be found in physical media and on TV.

People who create fake news use a few tricks that keep people believing their lies. They sprinkle in bits of truth. They also use fake sources that sound official and statements from sketchy eyewitnesses.

How to Spot Fake News

Knowing how to spot fake news is a great skill. Red flags include using emotional headlines, not citing credible sources, and making far-fetched promises.

If you want to be positive that what you're seeing is true, make sure you read more than just the headline. You can also look up the writer or the content creator spreading the

Having a good education goes a long way when it comes to being able to spot fake news.

IN THE SPOTLIGHT

Meet the Fact-Checkers

Fact-checkers are research experts. They look high and low to find accurate information. These people are dedicated to finding the truth, even when that means telling everyone that something is false. Sometimes they are college research students, and other times they are professionals in their field. Fact-checkers tell you what they found about a story, where they found it, and any differences in information that might be important to the story.

information. It's a good idea to check the sources they cited to see if they are real and reliable.

Fact-Checking Tools

With today's technology, it is easier than ever to double-check news sources. This can help decide if a news story, picture, or claim is fake.

Some sites have online fact-checking tools available. These are great to use when you aren't sure about something. The easiest way to find them is to do an online search for "fact check tools." These search tools, such as those available from Google Toolbox or FactCheck.org, can help you research sources to see which are most reliable.

Fact checking the information provided by a source is important for identifying fake news.

Comparing Sources

If you're wondering whether a piece of information might be fake news, make sure to compare it to more than one source. Make this a habit whether you're writing a report, making an important decision, or evaluating the latest viral video on the internet. You can use different sources to verify facts, including websites, books, magazines, and even eyewitness accounts.

Books are a good resource to use to verify information from an online source.

The ability to find true information in a sea of fake news is an important skill to develop.

CHAPTER THREE

USING CRITICAL THINKING SKILLS

Critical thinking skills are helpful for evaluating online sources. These are skills that help you question and analyze information before you believe it. Does something seem too bizarre to be true? This can often be a sign that the information is not from a credible source. It's always a good idea to double-check.

Who Wrote This?

Ask yourself who wrote or created the story you're being told. Is it a reliable person? Whether you're questioning the author of a science article or a kid at school who is spreading stories about a teacher, use your critical thinking skills to help you decide.

Here are a few things to be on the lookout for. Does the writer have experience in the subject? Do they have firsthand knowledge or relevant training? Have they written other articles or stories that are true?

Using critical thinking skills can help to figure out if a source should be trusted.

Why Was This Written?

Next, ask yourself why this person wrote this content. Does the author have something to gain from this story, such as money or votes? Are they reporting all sides of the story, or is someone's experience being left out?

If a source is trying to make you believe something that is slightly or completely untrue, it brings all of their stories into question. This means the "why" is very important!

Read information carefully to find clues that can tell you if it is true or false.

Question Everything

If you've looked at who wrote a story and why they wrote it, you might have found some information to be a bit questionable. Now what?

Dig a little deeper. Research the background of the story and any sources that are cited. Look for differences between this story and others about the subject. That can give you a clue about the truth.

Balancing Different Viewpoints

Sometimes a story might seem false to you, but someone in a different situation may not see it that way. A popular example is the number six and the number nine. If you draw the number six and look at it straight on, you can see the six.

LOOK FOR BALANCE!

A balanced point of view is important in all areas of life. Diversity in books, movies, education, and business promotes understanding and empathy for all cultures!

But if you flip the paper upside down, you see the number nine. So if one person sees a six and one person sees a nine, who is right? Who is wrong?

Understanding someone's point of view might help you to see how they view an issue.

Before determining whether a claim is false, ask yourself if it could be true from a different perspective. This can help us avoid bias or prejudice.

Using critical thinking skills will make it easier to decide to say yes or no to accepting an online source.

CHAPTER FOUR

RESPONSIBLE USE OF ONLINE INFORMATION

Using online sources should always be done responsibly. What does this mean for online news and information?

Plagiarism and Copyright

Did you know that pictures and information you find online actually belong to someone? The owner is usually the creator of the content. Copyright laws protect this content. Using or spreading it without permission can be illegal.

Sometimes people use content without permission, but they give credit to the author or creator. As long as the content is not being used to make money, this is generally OK. This is called citing your source.

Taking someone else's work and saying it is your own is called plagiarism. Never take something created by someone else and try to pass it off as your own. This can get you in trouble, such as getting a zero on an assignment or even getting expelled from school.

Copying information and pasting it into your assignment without citing it is considered to be plagiarism.

Creating Your Own Content

Do you want to create your own content? Maybe you have a school project, or maybe you are in a creative mood. You can use online sources to help you get started!

Tools like AI content generators can be fun to try out. But be sure to take what these generators give you and edit it to make it your own. Information from AI sources can be unreliable, so you will need to fact-check it.

If you ever need to use pieces of someone else's work, be sure to give them proper credit by citing your source. You can do this by adding a note to tell your audience where the content came from, and who created it.

Instead of trying to imitate or copy someone else's work, try to tap into your own creativity.

Using Information and Staying Safe Online

We should all do our best to share only true and helpful information. Just because we see something sensational online doesn't mean we should believe it. It is irresponsible to share news that can't be proven to be true.

If a website asks for personal information before granting access, you should leave that site. Always check the URL and make sure it starts with "https" and doesn't say "unsecure."

Watch for the warning signs that a website may be unsafe.

These tips will keep you away from sites that will likely be unreliable!

The sources we have discussed are amazing tools. Knowing how to use them is a must. As long as we are able to see the difference between unreliable and credible sources, use critical thinking skills when approaching new information, and research responsibly, we can be confident in the accuracy of the information.

Most smartphones will warn you if a site you are trying to access is unsafe or unsecure.

When presenting information, it's your responsibility to do all you can to make sure that it is fair and accurate.

GLOSSARY

bias: errors in a study or judgment that lead to unfair or wrong outcomes

cite: to quote or refer to something by name

credible: something good, believable, or trustworthy

copyright: the legal right to a creative work

empathy: the act of understanding or sharing the feelings of someone else

eyewitness: someone who saw something happen firsthand

news outlet: an organization that gathers news and spreads it to the public with websites, TV programs, or newspapers

plagiarism: the act of copying from someone and calling it one's own

prejudice: disliking someone or something without good reason

research: purposeful work taken to increase one's knowledge in a given subject

LEARN MORE

Britannica Kids: Primary Source
https://kids.britannica.com/kids/article/primary-source/629043

Carser, A. R. *What is Fake News?* San Diego: BrightPoint, 2023.

Grant, Joyce. *Can You Believe It?: How to Spot Fake News and Find the Facts*. Toronto: Kids Can Press, 2022.

Gravel, Elise. *Killer Underwear Invasion!: How to Spot Fake News, Disinformation & Conspiracy Theories*. San Francisco: Chronicle Books, 2022.

Kiddle: Digital Citizenship Facts for Kids
https://kids.kiddle.co/Digital_citizen

National Geographic Kids: How to be an Expert Fact-Checker
https://kids.nationalgeographic.com/homework-help/article/how-to-be-an-expert-fact-checker

News For Kids: Fake News
https://newsforkids.net/fastfacts/fake-news/

Oxlade, Chris. *Computer Science for Curious Kids: An Illustrated Introduction to Software Programming, Artificial Intelligence, Cyber Security, and More!* London, England: Arcturus, 2023.

INDEX

PHOTO ACKNOWLEDGMENTS

Image credits: InFocus.ee/Shutterstock, p. 5; Rawpixel/Shutterstock, p. 7; Santiparp Wattanaporn/Shutterstock, p. 8; BearFotos/Shutterstock, p. 10; FREEPIK2/Shutterstock, p. 11; Thomas Bethge/Shutterstock, p. 13; Arya J/Shutterstock, p. 15; Jirapong Manustrong/Shutterstock, p. 16; Roman Samborskyi/Shutterstock, p. 17; Whale Design/Shutterstock, p. 19; iQoncept/Shutterstock, p. 20; Sylverarts Vectors/Shutterstock, p. 21; mirzamlk/Shutterstock, p. 22; Feng Yu/Shutterstock, p. 23; Denis Junker/Shutterstock, p. 25; Pixelvario/Shutterstock, p. 26; Edaccor/Shutterstock p. 27; Fedorovekb/Shutterstock, p. 28; Monkey Business Images/Shutterstock, p. 29; Just dance/Shutterstock, p. 31. Cover image: Ground Picture/Shutterstock.